The
★ ★
UNITED
STATES
PRESIDENTS

John
TYLER

Megan M. Gunderson

Big Buddy Books
An Imprint of Abdo Publishing
abdopublishing.com

abdopublishing.com

Published by Abdo Publishing, a division of ABDO, PO Box 398166, Minneapolis, Minnesota 55439.
Copyright © 2017 by Abdo Consulting Group, Inc. International copyrights reserved in all countries. No part of this book may be reproduced in any form without written permission from the publisher. Big Buddy Books™ is a trademark and logo of Abdo Publishing.

Printed in the United States of America, North Mankato, Minnesota
062016
092016

Design: Sarah DeYoung, Mighty Media, Inc.
Production: Mighty Media, Inc.
Editor: Lauren Kukla
Cover Photograph: Getty Images
Interior Photographs: Alamy (p. 11); Corbis (pp. 25, 29); Getty Images (pp. 6, 13, 15, 19, 21); iStockphoto (p. 17); Library of Congress (pp. 5, 6, 7, 9, 23); Picture History (p. 27)

Cataloging-in-Publication Data

Names: Gunderson, Megan M., author.
Title: John Tyler / by Megan M. Gunderson.
Description: Minneapolis, MN : Abdo Publishing, [2017] | Series: United States presidents | Includes bibliographical references and index.
Identifiers: LCCN 2015957501 | ISBN 9781680781205 (lib. bdg.) | ISBN 9781680775402 (ebook)
Subjects: LCSH: Tyler, John, 1790-1862--Juvenile literature. | Presidents--United States--Biography--Juvenile literature. | United States--Politics and government--1841-1845--Juvenile literature.
Classification: DDC 973.5/8092 [B]--dc23
LC record available at http://lccn.loc.gov/2015957501

Contents

John Tyler

John Tyler was elected vice president in 1840. William H. Harrison was president. However, one month after taking office, President Harrison died. The US **Constitution** was unclear about what should happen next.

Some people thought the vice president should officially become the next president. Tyler agreed. So, he took the presidential **oath** of office. Tyler accomplished much as president. Then, after just one term, he left office.

Timeline

1790

On March 29, John Tyler was born in Charles City County, Virginia.

1825

Tyler became governor of Virginia.

1827

Tyler was elected to the US Senate.

1816

Tyler was elected to the US House of **Representatives**.

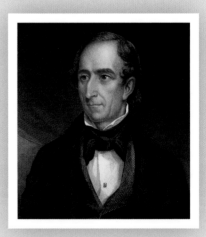

1841

On April 4, President Harrison died. Tyler became the tenth US president on April 6.

1840

Tyler was elected vice president under William H. Harrison.

1861

The **American Civil War** began. Tyler was elected to the **Confederate** House of **Representatives**.

1862

On January 18, John Tyler died.

7

Virginia Childhood

John Tyler was born on March 29, 1790, in Charles City County, Virginia. He was born on a large farm called Greenway. John's parents were John Tyler and Mary Armistead. John's father was a judge. The Tylers had eight children.

★ FAST FACTS ★

Born: March 29, 1790

Wives: Letitia Christian (1790–1842), Julia Gardiner (1820–1889)

Children: 15

Political Party: Whig

Age at Inauguration: 51

Years Served: 1841–1845

Vice President: None

Died: January 18, 1862, age 71

John's childhood home, Greenway, is just south of Virginia's capital, Richmond.

School Days

In 1802, John entered the College of William and Mary in Williamsburg, Virginia. He finished school in 1807. John then studied law with his father.

In 1808, John's father became governor of Virginia. So, he moved to Virginia's capital, Richmond. John went with his father.

John continued studying law in Richmond. He also joined a club to practice arguing cases. In 1809, John became a **lawyer**.

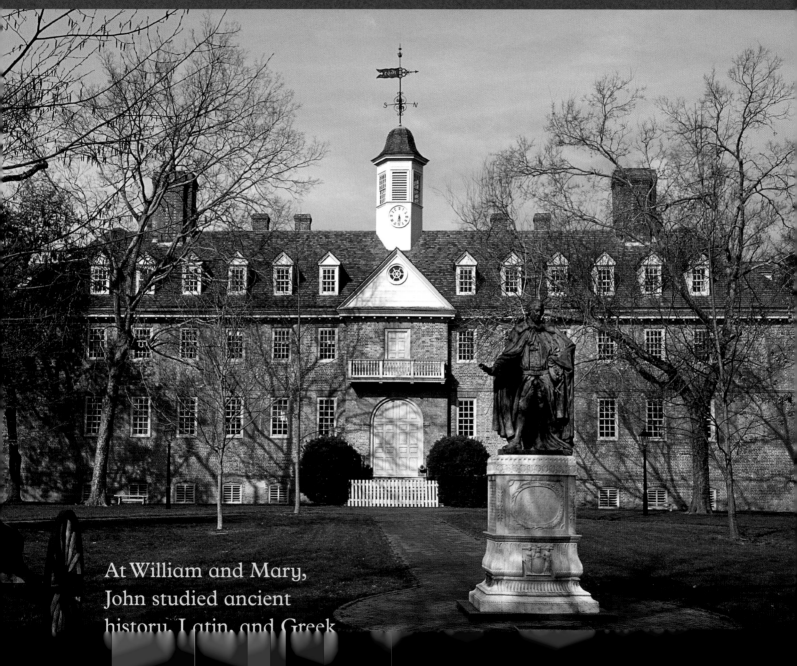

At William and Mary,
John studied ancient
history, Latin, and Greek

Family Man

Tyler quickly became a successful **lawyer**. Yet he was also interested in government. In 1811, Tyler was elected to the Virginia House of **Delegates**.

The next year, the **War of 1812** started. Tyler helped with this struggle. In 1813, he led a company of **militia** men. They guarded Richmond in case the British attacked.

That same year, Tyler married Letitia Christian. The couple lived at Greenway. They went on to have eight children.

Tyler had grown up just a few miles from Letitia's family.

Congressman Tyler

In 1816, Tyler was elected to the US House of **Representatives**. There, he voted against the Missouri **Compromise** of 1820. This bill decided how far slavery could spread in the country.

Tyler was a slave owner. He also felt the national government should not concern itself with slavery. Still, the compromise passed.

Tyler worked in Congress for four years. He left in 1821 due to poor health. When his health improved, he returned to the Virginia House of **Delegates** in 1823.

Tyler's excellent speaking skills helped him in his career.

Senator Tyler

In 1825, Tyler became Virginia's governor. He was elected to the US Senate two years later. At the time, Andrew Jackson was president. He opposed the Bank of the United States. So, Jackson took government money from it.

Tyler was not in favor of the bank either. But he felt Jackson did not have the power to remove the money. So, in 1834, Tyler voted to **censure** Jackson. Virginia lawmakers told Tyler to change his vote. But he refused. Tyler quit the Senate in 1836.

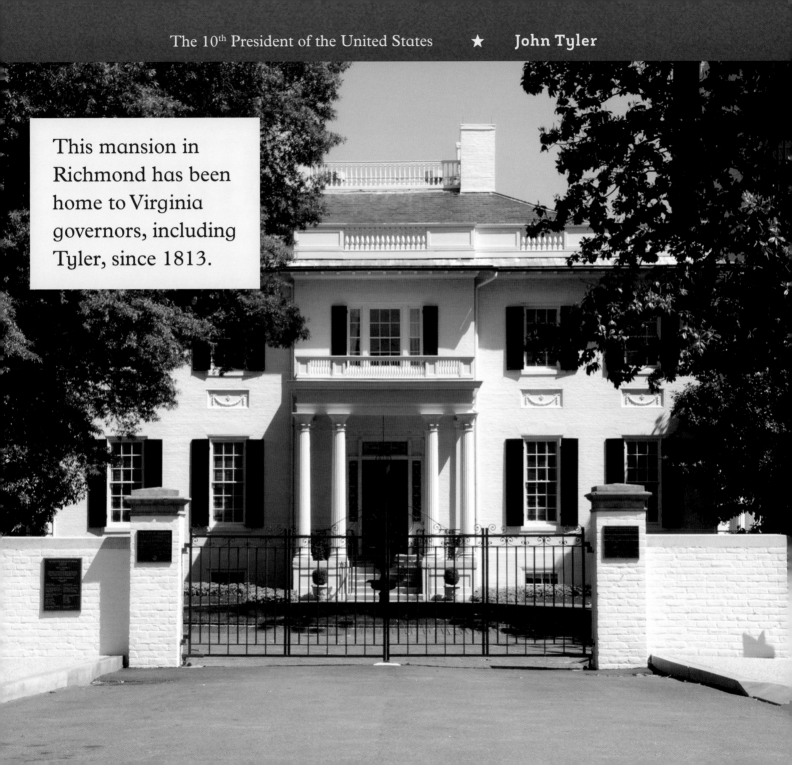

This mansion in Richmond has been home to Virginia governors, including Tyler, since 1813.

Whig Candidate

In 1834, the **Whig Party** formed. The Whigs opposed President Jackson. The Whig Party liked Tyler because he had been against Jackson.

In 1839, the Whigs chose William H. Harrison to run for president. Harrison was a hero of the American West. The Whigs hoped he could win the 1840 election.

However, the Whigs also needed Southern votes to win. Many Southerners liked Tyler. So, the Whigs asked him to run for vice president.

Tyler also ran for vice president in 1836, but he lost.

Vice President

The 1840 campaign was unusual. Both sides avoided talking about government problems. Instead, the parties used **slogans** and songs to get votes.

Harrison's nickname was "Old Tippecanoe." So, the **Whig** campaign slogan was "Tippecanoe and Tyler Too." The Whigs won the election!

On March 4, 1841, Harrison took office. Sadly, he got very sick soon after becoming president. President Harrison died on April 4, 1841.

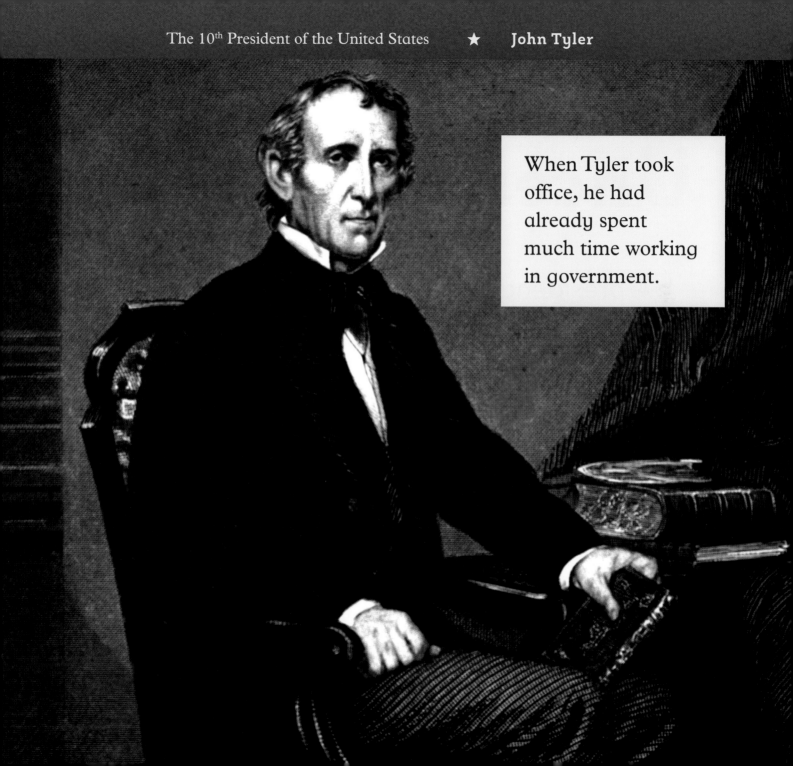

When Tyler took office, he had already spent much time working in government.

Uncertainty

A president had never died in office before. The **Constitution** was unclear about what should happen. Tyler's **cabinet** and other leaders thought the vice president should act as president. Others said the vice president should actually become president.

Tyler believed it was his right to become president. So, on April 6, 1841, Tyler took the presidential **oath** of office. Then, Congress officially recognized his right to be president. The cabinet agreed.

Tyler's actions set the course for future vice presidents. They, too, would become president if the president died.

President Tyler

As president, Tyler often disagreed with Congress. Early on, Congress passed two bills that would help form a new national bank. Tyler **vetoed** both of them.

After this, all but one member of Tyler's **cabinet** quit. They hoped to force him out. But Tyler just chose new cabinet members. Then, in 1841, **Whig** leaders removed him from the party.

Soon, Tyler faced personal changes. In September 1842, Letitia Tyler died. Two years later, Tyler married Julia Gardiner.

PRESIDENT TYLER'S CABINET

APRIL 6, 1841–MARCH 4, 1845

★ **STATE:** Daniel Webster,
Abel P. Upshur (from July 24, 1843),
John C. Calhoun (from April 1, 1844)

★ **TREASURY:** Thomas Ewing,
Walter Forward (from September 13, 1841),
John C. Spencer (from March 8, 1843),
George M. Bibb (from July 4, 1844)

★ **WAR:** John Bell,
John C. Spencer (from October 12, 1841),
James M. Porter (from March 8, 1843),
William Wilkins (from February 20, 1844)

★ **NAVY:** George Edmund Badger,
Abel P. Upshur (from October 11, 1841),
David Henshaw (from July 24, 1843),
Thomas W. Gilmer (from February 19, 1844),
John Y. Mason (from March 26, 1844)

★ **ATTORNEY GENERAL:** John Jordan Crittenden,
Hugh S. Legaré (from September 20, 1841),
John Nelson (from July 1, 1843)

Despite these changes, Tyler also had many successes. In 1842, the government ended the **Second Seminole War**. Tyler signed bills making Florida a state and **annexing** Texas.

As president, Tyler also helped settle a land issue with Great Britain. This led to the Webster-Ashburton **Treaty**. It created the border between Maine and Canada.

Tyler also wished to improve trade relations with other countries. So, in 1844, the United States signed a treaty with China. The treaty opened trade between the two nations.

SUPREME COURT
★ APPOINTMENTS ★

Samuel Nelson: 1845

Tyler and his second wife, Julia, had seven children together.

Later Life

Tyler did not run for a second term. In 1844, he backed James K. Polk. Polk won the election. Tyler left office the following March.

In 1861, the **American Civil War** began. Tyler was elected to the **Confederate** House of **Representatives**. However, he never took office. John Tyler died on January 18, 1862.

Tyler accomplished much as president. He fought successfully to become president. John Tyler set the standard for future vice presidents.

When Tyler left the White House, his family moved to Sherwood Forest, Virginia.

Office of the President

Branches of Government

The US government has three branches. They are the executive, legislative, and judicial branches. Each branch has some power over the others. This is called a system of checks and balances.

★ **Executive Branch**

The executive branch enforces laws. It is made up of the president, the vice president, and the president's cabinet. The president represents the United States around the world. He or she also signs bills into law and leads the military.

★ **Legislative Branch**

The legislative branch makes laws, maintains the military, and regulates trade. It also has the power to declare war. This branch includes the Senate and the House of Representatives. Together, these two houses form Congress.

★ **Judicial Branch**

The judicial branch interprets laws. It is made up of district courts, courts of appeals, and the Supreme Court. District courts try cases. Sometimes people disagree with a trial's outcome. Then he or she may appeal. If a court of appeals supports the ruling, a person may appeal to the Supreme Court.

Qualifications for Office

To be president, a candidate must be at least 35 years old. The person must be a natural-born US citizen. He or she must also have lived in the United States for at least 14 years.

Electoral College

The US presidential election is an indirect election. Voters from each state choose electors. These electors represent their state in the Electoral College. Each elector has one electoral vote. Electors cast their vote for the candidate with the highest number of votes from people in their state. A candidate must receive the majority of Electoral College votes to win.

Term of Office

Each president may be elected to two four-year terms. The presidential election is held on the Tuesday after the first Monday in November. The president is sworn in on January 20 of the following year. At that time, he or she takes the oath of office.
It states:

> I do solemnly swear (or affirm) that I will faithfully execute the office of President of the United States, and will to the best of my ability, preserve, protect and defend the Constitution of the United States.

31

Line of Succession

The Presidential Succession Act of 1947 states who becomes president if the president cannot serve. The vice president is first in the line. Next are the Speaker of the House and the President Pro Tempore of the Senate. It may happen that none of these individuals is able to serve. Then the office falls to the president's cabinet members. They would take office in the order in which each department was created:

Secretary of State

Secretary of the Treasury

Secretary of Defense

Attorney General

Secretary of the Interior

Secretary of Agriculture

Secretary of Commerce

Secretary of Labor

Secretary of Health and Human Services

Secretary of Housing and Urban Development

Secretary of Transportation

Secretary of Energy

Secretary of Education

Secretary of Veterans Affairs

Secretary of Homeland Security

Benefits

★ While in office, the president receives a salary. It is $400,000 per year. He or she lives in the White House. The president also has 24-hour Secret Service protection.

★ The president may travel on a Boeing 747 jet. This special jet is called Air Force One. It can hold 70 passengers. It has kitchens, a dining room, sleeping areas, and more. Air Force One can fly halfway around the world before needing to refuel. It can even refuel in flight!

★ When the president travels by car, he or she uses Cadillac One. It is a Cadillac Deville that has been modified. The car has heavy armor and communications systems. The president may even take Cadillac One along when visiting other countries.

★ The president also travels on a helicopter. It is called Marine One. It may also be taken along when the president visits other countries.

★ Sometimes the president needs to get away with family and friends. Camp David is the official presidential retreat. It is located in Maryland. The US Navy maintains the retreat. The US Marine Corps keeps it secure. The camp offers swimming, tennis, golf, and hiking.

★ When the president leaves office, he or she receives lifetime Secret Service protection. He or she also receives a yearly pension of $203,700. The former president also receives money for office space, supplies, and staff.

PRESIDENTS AND THEIR TERMS

PRESIDENT	PARTY	TOOK OFFICE	LEFT OFFICE	TERMS SERVED	VICE PRESIDENT
George Washington	None	April 30, 1789	March 4, 1797	Two	John Adams
John Adams	Federalist	March 4, 1797	March 4, 1801	One	Thomas Jefferson
Thomas Jefferson	Democratic-Republican	March 4, 1801	March 4, 1809	Two	Aaron Burr, George Clinton
James Madison	Democratic-Republican	March 4, 1809	March 4, 1817	Two	George Clinton, Elbridge Gerry
James Monroe	Democratic-Republican	March 4, 1817	March 4, 1825	Two	Daniel D. Tompkins
John Quincy Adams	Democratic-Republican	March 4, 1825	March 4, 1829	One	John C. Calhoun
Andrew Jackson	Democrat	March 4, 1829	March 4, 1837	Two	John C. Calhoun, Martin Van Buren
Martin Van Buren	Democrat	March 4, 1837	March 4, 1841	One	Richard M. Johnson
William H. Harrison	Whig	March 4, 1841	April 4, 1841	Died During First Term	John Tyler
John Tyler	Whig	April 6, 1841	March 4, 1845	Completed Harrison's Term	Office Vacant
James K. Polk	Democrat	March 4, 1845	March 4, 1849	One	George M. Dallas
Zachary Taylor	Whig	March 5, 1849	July 9, 1850	Died During First Term	Millard Fillmore

PRESIDENT	PARTY	TOOK OFFICE	LEFT OFFICE	TERMS SERVED	VICE PRESIDENT
Millard Fillmore	Whig	July 10, 1850	March 4, 1853	Completed Taylor's Term	Office Vacant
Franklin Pierce	Democrat	March 4, 1853	March 4, 1857	One	William R.D. King
James Buchanan	Democrat	March 4, 1857	March 4, 1861	One	John C. Breckinridge
Abraham Lincoln	Republican	March 4, 1861	April 15, 1865	Served One Term, Died During Second Term	Hannibal Hamlin, Andrew Johnson
Andrew Johnson	Democrat	April 15, 1865	March 4, 1869	Completed Lincoln's Second Term	Office Vacant
Ulysses S. Grant	Republican	March 4, 1869	March 4, 1877	Two	Schuyler Colfax, Henry Wilson
Rutherford B. Hayes	Republican	March 3, 1877	March 4, 1881	One	William A. Wheeler
James A. Garfield	Republican	March 4, 1881	September 19, 1881	Died During First Term	Chester Arthur
Chester Arthur	Republican	September 20, 1881	March 4, 1885	Completed Garfield's Term	Office Vacant
Grover Cleveland	Democrat	March 4, 1885	March 4, 1889	One	Thomas A. Hendricks
Benjamin Harrison	Republican	March 4, 1889	March 4, 1893	One	Levi P. Morton
Grover Cleveland	Democrat	March 4, 1893	March 4, 1897	One	Adlai E. Stevenson
William McKinley	Republican	March 4, 1897	September 14, 1901	Served One Term, Died During Second Term	Garret A. Hobart, Theodore Roosevelt

PRESIDENT	PARTY	TOOK OFFICE	LEFT OFFICE	TERMS SERVED	VICE PRESIDENT
Theodore Roosevelt	Republican	September 14, 1901	March 4, 1909	Completed McKinley's Second Term, Served One Term	Office Vacant, Charles Fairbanks
William Taft	Republican	March 4, 1909	March 4, 1913	One	James S. Sherman
Woodrow Wilson	Democrat	March 4, 1913	March 4, 1921	Two	Thomas R. Marshall
Warren G. Harding	Republican	March 4, 1921	August 2, 1923	Died During First Term	Calvin Coolidge
Calvin Coolidge	Republican	August 3, 1923	March 4, 1929	Completed Harding's Term, Served One Term	Office Vacant, Charles Dawes
Herbert Hoover	Republican	March 4, 1929	March 4, 1933	One	Charles Curtis
Franklin D. Roosevelt	Democrat	March 4, 1933	April 12, 1945	Served Three Terms, Died During Fourth Term	John Nance Garner, Henry A. Wallace, Harry S. Truman
Harry S. Truman	Democrat	April 12, 1945	January 20, 1953	Completed Roosevelt's Fourth Term, Served One Term	Office Vacant, Alben Barkley
Dwight D. Eisenhower	Republican	January 20, 1953	January 20, 1961	Two	Richard Nixon
John F. Kennedy	Democrat	January 20, 1961	November 22, 1963	Died During First Term	Lyndon B. Johnson
Lyndon B. Johnson	Democrat	November 22, 1963	January 20, 1969	Completed Kennedy's Term, Served One Term	Office Vacant, Hubert H. Humphrey
Richard Nixon	Republican	January 20, 1969	August 9, 1974	Completed First Term, Resigned During Second Term	Spiro T. Agnew, Gerald Ford

PRESIDENT	PARTY	TOOK OFFICE	LEFT OFFICE	TERMS SERVED	VICE PRESIDENT
Gerald Ford	Republican	August 9, 1974	January 20, 1977	Completed Nixon's Second Term	Nelson A. Rockefeller
Jimmy Carter	Democrat	January 20, 1977	January 20, 1981	One	Walter Mondale
Ronald Reagan	Republican	January 20, 1981	January 20, 1989	Two	George H.W. Bush
George H.W. Bush	Republican	January 20, 1989	January 20, 1993	One	Dan Quayle
Bill Clinton	Democrat	January 20, 1993	January 20, 2001	Two	Al Gore
George W. Bush	Republican	January 20, 2001	January 20, 2009	Two	Dick Cheney
Barack Obama	Democrat	January 20, 2009	January 20, 2017	Two	Joe Biden

"**We are in the enjoyment of all the blessings of civil and religious liberty.**" John Tyler

★ WRITE TO THE PRESIDENT ★

You may write to the president at:
The White House
1600 Pennsylvania Avenue NW
Washington, DC 20500

You may e-mail the president at:
comments@whitehouse.gov

Glossary

American Civil War—the war between the Northern and Southern states from 1861 to 1865.

annex—to take land and add it to a nation.

cabinet—a group of advisers chosen by the president to lead government departments.

censure (SEHNT-shuhr)—to officially show disapproval.

compromise—an agreement reached after each side gives up something.

Confederate—of or related to the group of Southern states that declared independence during the American Civil War.

constitution (kahnt-stuh-TOO-shuhn)—the basic laws that govern a country or a state.

delegate—someone who represents other people at a meeting or in a lawmaking group.

lawyer (LAW-yuhr)—a person who gives people advice on laws or represents them in court.

militia (muh-LIH-shuh)—people who help the army in times of need, they are not soldiers.

oath—a formal promise or statement.

representative—someone chosen in an election to act or speak for the people who voted for him or her.

Second Seminole War—from 1835 to 1842. A battle between the Seminole Native Americans and the US government to remove the Seminole from their Florida lands.

slogan—a word or a phrase used to express a position, a stand, or a goal.

treaty—an agreement made between two or more groups.

veto—the right of one member of a decision-making group to stop an action by the group. In the US government, the president can veto bills passed by Congress. But Congress can override the president's veto if two-thirds of its members vote to do so.

War of 1812—a war between the United States and England from 1812 to 1815.

Whig Party—a US political party active between 1834 and 1854.

★ WEBSITES ★

To learn more about the US Presidents, visit **booklinks.abdopublishing.com**. These links are routinely monitored and updated to provide the most current information available.

Index